the art of
EGYPT
---
under the
Pharaohs

by Shirley Glubok

Designed by Gerard Nook

Macmillan Publishing Co., Inc.
New York
Collier Macmillan Publishers
London

The author gratefully acknowledges the assistance of:
Thomas J. Logan, Associate Curator of Egyptian Art, The Metropolitan Museum of Art;
Dietrich Wildung, Director, Municipal Museum of Egyptian Art, Munich; *Lewis McNaught*,
British Museum; *Mina Roustayi*; *Stacy Stiffel*;
and especially the helpful cooperation of *Robert Bianchi*,
Associate Curator of Egyptian and Classical Art, The Brooklyn Museum.

10 9 8 7 6 5 4 3 2 1

Library of Congress Cataloging in Publication Data
Glubok, Shirley.   The art of Egypt under the pharaohs.
Summary: Surveys Egyptian art from Dynasty 1 through the Ptolemaic
Period, approximately 3200 through 30 B.C., discussing it
in terms of the history and culture of the period.
1. Art, Egyptian—Juvenile literature. [1. Art, Egyptian]
I. Nook, Gerard. II. Title. N5350.G63 709'.32 79-23336 ISBN 0-02-736470-4

PRECEDING PAGES: Wall painting from the tomb of Sennedjem, dynasty 19,
about 1340–1195 B.C., photograph by Egyptian Expedition,
The Metropolitan Museum of Art

Dynasty 1,
about 3200 B.C.,
photograph
by Max Hirmer

Egypt is a hot, dry country in northeastern Africa. The great Nile River runs through the land. The Nile begins at Lake Victoria, in the mountains near the Equator, then runs northward. As the Nile flows through Egypt, there is barren desert on either side of the narrow river valley. This natural barrier kept the ancient Egyptians apart from their neighbors and protected them from their enemies. In the north of Egypt the river spreads out into many branches and empties into the Mediterranean Sea. This fertile area is known as the Delta.

It almost never rains in Egypt, but the soil is rich all along the banks of the river. In ancient times the Nile rose and overflowed each spring when snows melted and rains fell in the south. These yearly floods carried fertile topsoil which was deposited in the river valley, so the Egyptians could be farmers with a settled way of life. One of the earliest and longest lasting civilizations the world has known was developed in the Nile valley.

The Nile runs from south to north, so the southern part of the country is called Upper Egypt and the northern part Lower Egypt. In prehistoric times, these were separate kingdoms. Then, about five thousand years ago, the North was conquered by the South under the leadership of King Menes, and Egypt was united. Around this time a system of writing and a calendar were developed by the Egyptians, and their recorded history began. The carving on the stone tablet above shows Menes capturing a prisoner from Lower Egypt. Menes became the first Pharaoh; Dynasty 1 began with his reign.

Dynasty 4, about 2680–2565 B.C., Cairo Museum, photograph The Metropolitan Museum of Art

A dynasty is a series of kings who are members of the same family. In Egyptian history there were thirty-one dynastic periods, covering more than three thousand years. The dynasties are grouped into the Archaic Period, the Old, Middle and New Kingdoms, and the Late Period. After each of the Kingdoms there were Intermediate Periods, which were unsettled times.

Chephren was a king, or Pharaoh, of Dynasty 4 of the Old Kingdom. In the statue at left, Horus, the god of the sky who takes the form of a hawk, spreads his wings to protect the king. The wings of Horus spanned the heavens, and his eyes were the sun and the moon. The Egyptians believed in many gods. The Pharaoh was thought to be the son of Ra, the sun god, and he himself was worshiped as a god.

Chephren built a pyramid at Giza, in the desert, near the modern city of Cairo. The pyramids, which were the tombs of royalty, are colossal stone structures. Each pyramid had a mortuary temple for funeral services at its base and a "valley temple" on the edge of the desert next to the fertile land of the Nile valley. The two temples were connected by a causeway, a covered road that was used for the king's funeral procession.

A giant sphinx guards the entrance to the causeway on Chephren's sacred burial grounds. The huge stone figure with the head of the Pharaoh and the body of a lion showed that the king was as strong as a lion. This great sphinx was carved from a natural rock that rises out of the desert; its front paws were built up of smaller blocks of stone.

Photograph by Dietrich Wildung

The statue at left of the Pharaoh Mycerinus and his queen, Khamerernebty, is from this king's valley temple at his pyramid in Giza. The queen has her arm around the king, an unusual pose in royal statues. Her face looks like his because it was the custom for the artist to make everyone look the same as the Pharaoh.

Mycerinus wears a headdress of linen cloth, a false, ceremonial beard and a short kilt, or piece of cloth that wraps around the waist and laps over in front. His wife wears the tight everyday dress of Egyptian ladies at this time.

Mycerinus's pyramid is only 216 feet high. It is the smallest of the three kings' pyramids at Giza. The little pyramids in front of it were built for his relatives.

Dynasty 4, Museum of Fine Arts, Boston,
Harvard-MFA Expedition

Photograph by Max Hirmer

The pyramid of Chephren, in the middle, looks like the tallest because it was built on higher ground. But the one built for Cheops, Chephren's father, is the largest. This "Great Pyramid" is about 480 feet high and covers nearly thirteen acres. More than two million blocks of stone were used; some of them weighed as much as fifteen tons. These huge blocks of stone were cut with small tools made of stone or copper.

A supply of good stone could be found to the south of Giza. Large blocks were taken from the quarry and moved on sledges, which are like sleds with wide wooden runners. Then they were floated down the river to Giza at flood time. Ramps of mud brick were built so that the stones could be dragged up the sides of the pyramid as it grew taller.

oblemen and officials were buried in mastabas, rectangular stone structures with sloping sides and flat roofs. Mastabas were grouped in rows close to the pyramids so the noblemen could be near their Pharaoh after death, as they were in life. Ancient Egyptians enjoyed life, and they believed that life could continue after death and be the same as it had been on earth. Egyptian art is based on this belief in the afterlife.

Everyone was thought to have a "ba," or soul. The ba resided in the body during the person's lifetime, and at the moment of death it flew away in the form of a human-headed bird. In order for life to continue after death, the ba needed to have a dwelling place. It could return to the dead person's body in the tomb, but first the body had to be preserved in a lifelike form so the ba could recognize it. Great care was taken to have the body "mummified" by drying it out, preserving it with chemicals and wrapping it in many layers of linen. Then the mummy was put into one or more mummy cases in the form of a person, which were enclosed in a sarcophagus, or large rectangular coffin.

The burial chamber in a mastaba was at the bottom of a deep shaft underneath the structure. The mastaba also had a room with a false door. It was believed that the ba could magically pass through the false door to enjoy food and other offerings that were left in front of the tomb.

The figure at right is from a false door in the mastaba of Nykauhor, who was a judge. Before being painted, the figure was carved out of the stone by cutting away the background to make a "raised relief." In Egyptian reliefs and paintings everything was represented from the angle that could be seen most clearly; so the head and legs of a person were shown in profile, or side view, while the body and eyes were shown full front. In this painted relief, Nykauhor seems to have two right feet.

Walls in the rooms of mastabas were painted with scenes of everyday life. The geese below have clearly marked feathers; the bits of grass represent plants in the marshes of the river. The painting is from the mastaba of Nefermaat, a son of King Sneferu.

Dynasty 5, about 2565–2420 B.C., The Metropolitan Museum of Art, Rogers Fund

Dynasty 4, Cairo Museum, photograph by Max Hirmer

Dynasty 4, Cairo Museum, photograph by Max Hirmer

These limestone statues were found in the mastaba of another son of King Sneferu, Prince Rahotep, who was commander of the archers. His wife, Lady Nofret, was a member of the court. Egyptian statues usually were brightly painted, but on most statues the paint has worn off. The paint on these statues looks fresh, although it is more than four thousand years old. Rahotep's skin is dark and his wife's is light. Egyptian artists painted the skins of men reddish brown, while the women were painted light yellow. Men were warriors and hunters; they spent their days outdoors and would get tanned from the hot sun. Women stayed indoors so their skins were

Dynasty 6, about 2420–2260 B.C., Cairo Museum, photograph Werner Forman Archive, London

pale. The eyes of the statues were inlaid with rock crystal to make them look more lifelike.

A dwarf named Seneb, who was a tutor in the royal court, is seated cross-legged next to his wife in the limestone statue at left. Standing below Seneb are figures of his son and daughter. It was the custom to show children naked, with their fingers on their mouths, and to show a boy with a curl of hair hanging down one side of his head. In ancient Egypt, dwarfs were highly prized as personal servants and they often performed as temple dancers. The merry household god, Bes, was represented as a dwarf.

King Pepy II received a dwarf as a gift from an African Pygmy tribe. In the small alabaster statue at right, Pepy is represented as a fully grown king wearing the cloth headdress and ceremonial beard of the ruler, yet he is sitting on his mother's lap like a little boy. Pepy became king when he was six years old. He ruled Egypt for more than ninety years, until he was nearly one hundred years old. When he died Egypt was in a state of political confusion, and the Old Kingdom came to an end.

Dynasty 6, The Brooklyn Museum, Charles Edwin Wilbour Fund

The Pharaoh Sesostris I was a ruler of Dynasty 12 in the Middle Kingdom. The word "Pharaoh" comes from the Egyptian phrase "Per-aha," which means "Great House," or royal palace. The Hebrews were the first to use this name. In the Bible the ruler of Egypt is called "Pharaoh." The limestone statue at left was found in the burial chamber of Sesostris's pyramid. A statue was very important; it could take the place of the mummy in case the mummy was destroyed.

The ancient Egyptians believed that every person had an invisible twin, a spirit which was born with him and stayed with him throughout life. After death this spirit, or "ka," made its home in the tomb in a statue representing the dead person. To make certain that the ka would enter the statue, magic ceremonies were performed.

This statue of Sesostris has ideal, or perfect, features. Pharaohs were usually represented as strong, handsome young men, to provide a fit body in which the ka could dwell forever.

The black granite sphinx represents Amenemhat III. His stern face looks out from the strong lion's body. A sphinx usually wears the royal headcloth, but Amenemhat has the mane of a lion.

Dynasty 12, Cairo Museum, photograph Bildarchiv Foto Marburg

Dynasty 12, The Metropolitan Museum of Art, Rogers Fund and Henry Walters Gift

Another Middle Kingdom Pharaoh, Sesostris II, gave the pectoral, or chest ornament, at left to his daughter Princess Sithathoryunet. It is made of gold with more than three hundred tiny semiprecious stones separated by fine gold wires. Two falcons with disks of the sun god on their heads stand on either side of a kneeling figure that represents the god of years. Above the god an oval frame encloses figures that stand for the king's name in Egyptian hieroglyphs, or picture writing. The royal name in an oval frame is called a "cartouche." The scarab beetle in the cartouche represents eternal life. When the heart was removed in the mummification process, a stone "scarab" in the shape of a beetle was put in its place. The cross with a loop, called the "ankh," is the Egyptian sign of life. Taken together, the symbols mean, "The sun god has granted hundreds of thousands of years of life to Sesostris II."

In the carving at right another princess, Kawit, is shown with two servants. One of them pours a liquid for the princess while the other puts a hairpin in her curls. The princess holds a cup in one hand, a mirror in the other. Mirrors were made of shiny bronze. Kawit is wearing jewelry around her neck and on her ankles and wrist. Egyptian women liked to wear jewelry, to color their cheeks and fingernails and to paint the rims of their eyes with cosmetics made from minerals and oils. Eye makeup was thought to be protection against evil entering the body through the eyes.

The scene is from one side of the princess's stone sarcophagus, which enclosed her mummy cases. It is carved in "sunken relief," made by cutting into the surface to sink the image into the stone. The small figures in this relief are hieroglyphs.

Dynasty 11, about 2040–1990 B.C., Cairo Museum, photograph by Max Hirmer

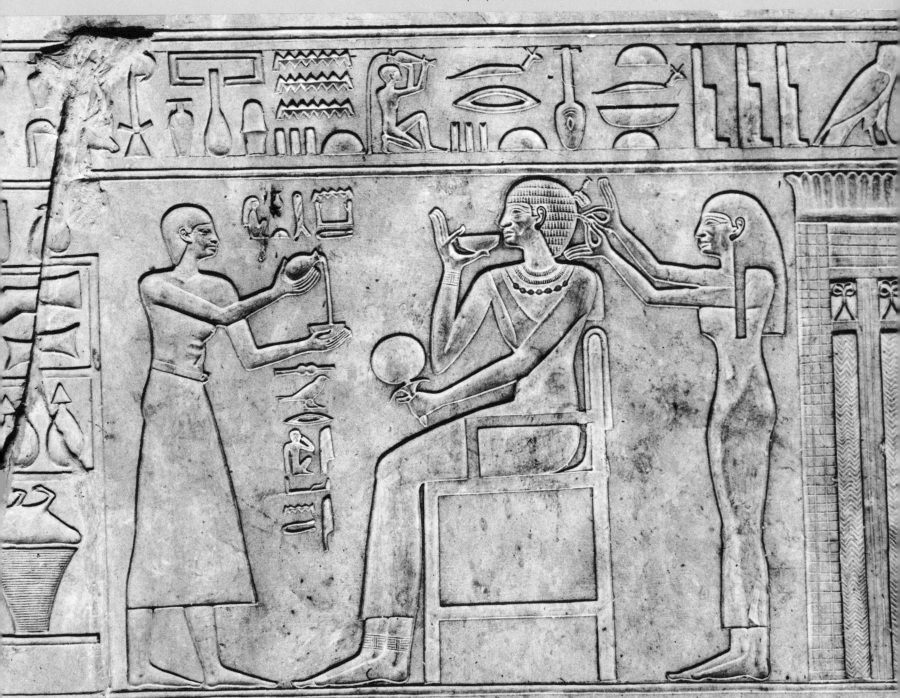

Little wooden figures of servants were sometimes placed in tombs. It was thought that the servants accompanied their master and could work for him in his afterlife.

The model of a granary below is from the tomb of Meketre, a high official to the king. Men are scooping up wheat and loading it into sacks, while others carry the sacks upstairs and dump the wheat into bins. Clerks, sitting cross-legged, keep count on scrolls of papyrus which are unrolled on their knees. Papyrus is a tall plant that grows in the marshes of the Nile. Its reeds, or stems, were used to make paper, which was called papyrus after the plant. The reeds were also tied together to make boats, and the roots were used for food. A story in the Bible tells about the baby Moses, who was hidden among papyrus reeds to save his life when the Pharaoh was killing the first-born in every

Dynasty 11, The
Metropolitan Museum
of Art, Rogers Fund and
Edward S. Harkness Gift

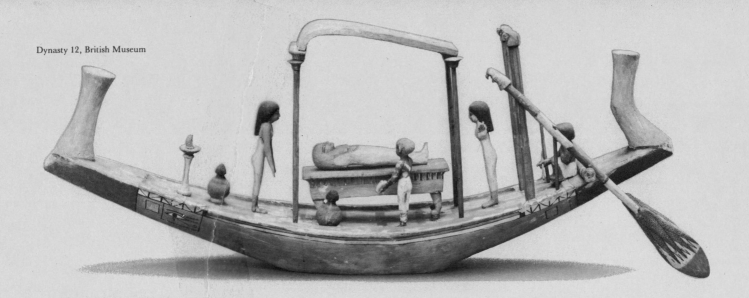

Hebrew family. Moses was saved when he was found by the Pharaoh's daughter.

People's mummified bodies were put on boats before being buried. It was thought that they sailed to a sacred place where their souls could pass directly into the Afterworld. In the wooden model above, the mummy of a woman is lying on a funeral chest, protected from the sun by a canopy. A workman steers with large oars.

Another wooden tomb figure represents a farmer with a simple plow drawn by two oxen. During Dynasty 11, when this figure was made, the Egyptians did not yet have horses. Several hundred years later, people from western Asia, known as the Hyksos, settled in Egypt and brought horses with them. For a time the Hyksos ruled Egypt.

When Egypt was taken over again by her own people, the country was reorganized, and the third great period of Egyptian history, known as the New Kingdom, began. During Dynasty 18, neighboring lands were conquered and Egypt became wealthier and stronger than she had ever been before. One of the great Pharaohs of this dynasty was Hatshepsut, the daughter of Tuthmosis I and wife of Tuthmosis II, who was also her half brother. It was common among Egyptian royalty for brothers to marry sisters, to strengthen their claim to the kingship. It also was common for fathers to marry their daughters, to keep the royal bloodline pure.

A king usually would have one or more principal wives and several minor wives as well. When Tuthmosis II died, Tuthmosis III, his son by a minor wife, should have become king. Since Tuthmosis III was a young child, Hatshepsut became regent, to rule until the boy was old enough. However, Hatshepsut seized full power for herself, adopted the royal titles of a king and had herself represented in the poses of a male ruler.

18

Dynasty 18, about 1570–1340 B.C., The Metropolitan
Museum of Art, Rogers Fund and Edward S. Harkness Gift

In the white limestone statue at left, Hatshepsut is wearing the royal headcloth of a male Pharaoh, yet she has the slender form of a beautiful woman. The statue was made for her funerary temple.

Hatshepsut died after ruling more than twenty years and Tuthmosis III was finally able to take over the throne. He was so angry with his stepmother that he had her statues broken up and her name erased from her monuments. Tuthmosis III was a military man, one of the greatest generals in history. He conquered Syria; the land of Canaan, which is now Israel; Mesopotamia, which is now Iraq; and parts of Africa. During his reign Egypt became a world power with a far-reaching empire.

The statue of Tuthmosis III at right is from Karnak, where a great temple was built to Amon, the chief god of Egypt. The king's ''prenomen,'' or throne name, is carved in a cartouche on the waistband of his kilt.

Dynasty 18, Cairo Museum, photograph by Max Hirmer

The "block statue" below represents Senmut, Hatshepsut's vizier, or chief minister, and tutor of Hatshepsut's daughter. Senmut is seated on the ground with his knees drawn up to his chin. The entire body of the statue is

Dynasty 18,
British Museum

shaped like a simple cube. A person's future in the afterlife depended on the safety of his statue because it was a home for his ka, so it was important that no part of the body should be broken off.

Senmut was the architect for Hatshepsut's funerary temple, which was set in the desert

against the great cliffs in Western Thebes. It is one of the most beautiful monuments in all Egypt. The holiest rooms were carved into the living rock of the cliffs. Terraces were planted with vines and trees from far-off lands. Hatshepsut's fleets sailed on the Red Sea to bring back rare plants for the garden. Most highly prized were the trees that bore incense, which was burned in the temple for its sweet smell. Inside, the walls were carved with scenes of the queen's birth, life and trading expeditions. Hatshepsut claimed that Amon was her father, and the temple was built in his honor.

Dynasty 18, British Museum

Amenhotep III also had a large funerary temple on the west bank of the Nile at Thebes. He built a palace nearby, where a lake was dug for the pleasure of his chief queen. In the palace was a great hall for the celebration of the king's jubilees, or royal festivals. This king is known for his love of luxury and is often called "Amenhotep the Magnificent." He did not care much for war or sports, but he liked to hunt fierce lions and capture wild bulls.

On the east bank of the Nile, he built a temple to Amon, which is now known as the Temple of Luxor. The head of Amenhotep III at left is from this temple. He is wearing the helmet of the Pharaoh, with the cobra over the forehead. The cobra was a sign of royalty. The sculptors of Amenhotep III carved a great many statues of him. Large statues were roughly cut out of boulders at the quarry. These boulders were taken to the temple where the work was finished by a team of sculptors.

Amenhotep III's chief queen was Tiy, a commoner with no royal blood. He was also married to several Asiatic princesses. Queen Tiy was a strong and active woman. She played an important part in the religion and politics of the kingdom and was the first queen whose name was included in the royal titles.

The small head above, made of boxwood, represents Tiy. Her eyes were inlaid with glass and she wears earrings of gold and lapis lazuli, a semiprecious stone. Tiy's wig is made of cloth that was covered with mud and wax.

In Dynasty 18 it became common to hollow tombs out of the limestone of the desert cliffs, in the hope that robbers would not find the mummies and the precious objects buried with them. A nobleman named Ramose had a splendid tomb cut out of rock on the west bank of the Nile at Thebes. Figures of Ramose and members of his family were carved in raised relief on the walls. Eyes were outlined in black paint to make them stand out. The figure at left represents Ramose. He was probably an old man when it was carved, but he looks like a handsome youth. He is wearing a necklace that was a gift from the king and a gown held up by narrow straps. The hieroglyphs give Ramose's name and list his titles.

Scenes of his funeral are painted on another wall in the tomb. The artists took more freedom in the wall paintings than in the relief carvings. The paintings express human feelings, which is rare in Egyptian art. Below, a group of grieving women is led by Ramose's wife Meriptah. At a funeral, professional mourners walked through the streets crying out and pouring dust on their heads. Women tore their garments and beat their bodies to show their grief. In this scene tears fall from the women's eyes as they mourn the dead nobleman. They have let their hair fall down their backs and have bared their breasts, which was the custom for mourners. The women appear in different poses, using a variety of gestures, and figures overlap each other.

Ramose was vizier of Upper Egypt. He served under Amenhotep III and for a time under Amenhotep IV also.

Amenhotep IV was a strange-looking man with an egg-shaped head, thick lips and a long chin, a thin neck, drooping shoulders and a pot belly. He had himself represented truthfully in this manner. His appearance set the style; his wife Nofretete and other members of the family were made to look like him. The sunken relief above was made for worship of the royal family in a private home. The king and queen are holding their daughters and kissing them. Ribbons flow from their tall crowns, and their bodies seem to sink into the cushions. The affectionate poses and the relaxed manner of the king and queen are unusual in Egyptian art.

At the top of the relief is the sun disk with rays ending in hands. Some of these rays hold the ankh, or sign of life, bringing life into the nostrils of the king and queen. This symbolizes that the sun is the giver of life. The state religion was controlled by the wealthy and powerful priests of Amon. Amenhotep IV broke away from the established religion and worshiped the Aten, or sun disk, as the only god, the supreme being who created the world and all living things. Other Egyptian gods took the form of a bird, an animal or a person, but the Aten only took the form of the sun disk.

The king, whose name meant ''Amon is satisfied,'' changed his name to Akhenaten, which means ''the spirit of the Aten,'' and moved the capital away from Thebes, home of the high priests of Amon. He built a new city in Middle Egypt called Akhetaten, or ''horizon of the Aten,'' known today as Tell el Amarna. It is said that he drove there in a golden chariot, and the rays of the sun shining on him pointed to the spot where his new city should be.

Akhenaten worshiped his god in the open air in a temple courtyard. He wrote songs to Aten which resemble the Hebrew psalms of David in the Bible: ''You arise beautiful in the horizon of heaven, O living Aten, beginning of life.''

Limestone relief from Tell el Amarna,
Dynasty 18, The Brooklyn Museum, Charles Edwin Wilbour Fund

27

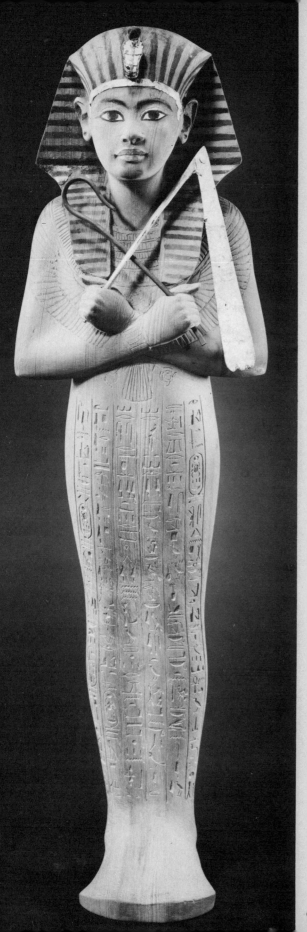

Akhenaten and Nofretete, whose name means "the beautiful woman has come," had six daughters and no sons. The eldest daughter married a half brother of the king named Semenkhkara, who shared the throne and ruled with Akhenaten as co-regent. The two regents died about the same time. Another half brother, called Tutankhaten, or "the living image of Aten," married Akhenaten's third daughter and became the next king. He was only nine years old when he ascended the throne. Tutankhaten left the new city of Akhetaten and moved his court back to the old capital at Thebes. He returned to the old religion of Amon and changed his name to Tutankhamon.

The young king is represented in the "shawabti" made of wood, at left. A shawabti is a little statue in the shape of a mummy that acted as a magic servant in the Afterworld. The face is a likeness of the dead person and the body is covered with the person's name and magic charms in hieroglyphs. The charms call on the shawabti to act as a substitute when Osiris, god of the dead, asks the deceased to work in the Fields of the Blessed. Tutankhamon's shawabti holds the crook and flail, which are signs of the king's godliness.

The jewel in the form of a human-headed bird is made of gold and semiprecious stones. It represents Tutankhamon's ba, or soul, and it was placed in the linen wrapping of his mummy.

This solid gold mask, with the royal cobra on the forehead and false beard on the chin, was placed over the face of Tutankhamon's mummy. It is inlaid with semiprecious stones and colored

Cairo Museum, photograph by John G. Ross

glass paste. Three coffins were placed over the mummy; the innermost was made of solid gold. The coffins were set into a stone sarcophagus and four wooden shrines were placed over it, one above the other, for extra protection.

Tutankhamon died when he was only about eighteen years old. His tomb was cut into the side of a cliff in the Valley of the Kings on the west bank of the Nile at Thebes. The west was considered the world of the dead, where the sun god descended every night, to be born again in the east in the morning. Kings usually lived on the east bank and were buried on the west bank of the river.

This painting is on the wall of the burial chamber in Tutankhamon's tomb. The figure farthest right is his uncle Ay, who was a high official. He managed affairs for the boy king and succeeded him to the throne. Ay is wearing the leopard skin of a priest and he is performing the "opening of the mouth" ceremony. This was the final ceremony in the funeral service before the mummy was lowered into the burial chamber. When the eyes and mouth of the mummy were touched by the priest, the dead person's sight, speech and movement were magically restored so he could see, speak and eat forever. Facing Ay is Tutankhamon transformed into Osiris, who is always shown in the form of a mummy with a tall crown. Osiris was a legendary king who died and was mummified, then was restored to life and became a god. It was thought that every dead king became Osiris and continued to reign over the realm of the dead. At the far left, Tutankhamon, followed by his ka, is embracing Osiris, with whom he has been united. The figures in the center of the painting are the young king and Nut, goddess of the sky.

The commander in chief of the army for Tutankhamon, named Horemheb, also had served Akhenaten and his father before him. He led successful military expeditions to the east into the land of Canaan and to the south into Nubia. Horemheb had entered the army as a royal scribe. Scribes were educated men and the only people who could read and write. He advanced to become the most powerful man in the land during the reign of Tutankhamon. When Ay died, Horemheb became king, even though he had no royal blood. As king he improved the laws to suppress crime and help the poor.

In the gray granite statue at left, Horemheb is seated cross-legged in the position of a scribe. He wears a long, pleated linen garment with flowing sleeves, which was the dress of

Dynasty 19, about
1340–1195 B.C.,
Egyptian Museum,
Turin, Italy,
photograph Alinari

a wealthy person at the time. His flabby stomach is also a sign of prosperity. Horemheb has unrolled his papyrus scroll on his knees and is composing a poem to Thoth, the god who was the inventor of writing. Thoth was the wisest of the gods; scribes often began their work with a prayer to him.

In Dynasties 19 and 20, eleven Pharaohs called themselves Ramesses. The second king by that name conquered the land of Canaan and went as far as northern Syria. He ruled sixty-seven years and lived to be more than ninety years old. In the seated statue at left, Ramesses II is holding the scepter, a symbol of kingship, and wearing the royal helmet. Ramesses's son, standing at his feet, is tiny, to show that he is less important than the king.

A courtyard at the Temple of Amon at Luxor was built for Ramesses II. His statues show him dressed in the manner of the Old Kingdom, in a short kilt and royal headcloth, with bare feet. Ramesses II had one of his temples carved out of a cliff at Abu Simbel. He also finished the construction of a hall with colossal columns at Karnak. And he built a great temple known as the Ramesseum on the west bank of the Nile at Thebes. The Bible tells of the Hebrew slaves who were oppressed by the Pharaoh and fled Egypt under

Dynasty 19, photograph about 1885

the leadership of Moses. It is believed that these Hebrew slaves who escaped from Egypt to the ''Promised Land'' of Canaan had been building the Ramesseum.

The rock-cut tomb of Nofretari, the favorite wife of Ramesses II, is in the Valley of the Queens in Western Thebes. The walls of the tomb were carved in raised relief and covered with a thick coat of plaster, then painted. At right, Nofretari is wearing a flowing white gown with a long sash, a broad jeweled collar and the vulture headdress of the queen mother. Hieroglyphs on the wall give the queen's titles and make statements about the gods.

The goddess Isis is welcoming Nofretari to the world of the dead and leading her to the sun god. Isis wears a tight gown with a pattern of beads. On her head is a crown with the royal cobra and the sun disk between the horns of a cow. A legend tells that Isis made the first cobra. When Ra's spittle fell on the dust, Isis molded the moist dust into a clay snake, put poison into it and hid it in the grass. The creature surprised Ra, who thought that all living things had been created by him. The cobra became the sacred snake of Egypt.

It was thought that scenes painted on the walls of tombs would become real by means of magic. In the wall painting below, Pashedu, a nobleman, is kneeling under a palm tree to drink from a sacred pool. It was believed that Pashedu would be transformed into a palm tree by drinking the sacred waters. The Egyptians thought that a dead person could also be transformed into an animal, a bird or a flower. The hieroglyphs which cover the wall are beautiful small drawings in themselves. Each of these picture-signs stands for a consonant, a group of consonants or the word for the object represented. There are no vowels in Egyptian hieroglyphic writing.

On the walls in the tomb of Sennedjem, another nobleman, he and his wife are working in the Fields of the Blessed, a land of eternal spring ruled by Osiris. It was believed that when a person died his heart was weighed in a balance scale against the "feather of truth" to determine whether his heart was pure. If it was not pure, the person was devoured by demons. But if he had done good deeds in his lifetime, he could live in the Fields of the Blessed with harvests that would go on forever.

At the top of the wall the sun god, in the form of a falcon, is making his trip across the heavens in a boat. Egyptians believed that the

Dynasty 20, about 1195–1085 B.C.,
photograph by Max Hirmer

sky was a sea and that beneath the earth there was another Nile. The sun sailed westward every day and then floated through the long, dark passage of the underground river before appearing again in the east in the early morning.

apyrus scrolls covered with magic spells and pictures were placed in the burial chamber to protect the dead person from evil demons and to enable him to enter and leave the tomb when he wished. Today these scrolls are commonly called the "Book of the Dead." In the Book of the Dead of the nobleman Nakht, he and his wife are worshiping Osiris before a pool in their garden. The pool is painted as if seen from above, while the trees and bushes surrounding it are seen from the sides. A fruit tree and a date palm stand in front of the house, which was made of sun-dried bricks. Ventilators on top of the flat roof would catch any cool breeze.

Nakht's wife is holding two lotus flowers and a sistrum, or rattle, with the head of Hathor, the cow goddess. This musical instrument made a jingling noise and was thought to attract the attention of the gods. On top of the couple's heavy wigs are cones of perfumed ointment which would smell sweet as it melted and trickled down their hair.

Figures of the gods of the Afterworld are represented on this mummy case of a noblewoman named Henettawy, the wife of a high priest of Amon. Women of high rank acted as priestesses in the temple of Amon, singing and playing musical instruments. Henettawy was a songstress of Amon. She lived during Dynasty 21, which was the beginning of the Third Intermediate Period.

Dynasty 21, about 1085–950 B.C.,
The Metropolitan Museum of Art, Rogers
Fund and Edward S. Harkness Gift

Dynasty 19, British Museum

The empire had been growing weaker during the late New Kingdom under the rule of a series of Ramesseses, and now the country was again divided. Troubled times followed. During Dynasty 21, kings ruled from Tanis in the Delta. One of the kings of this period sent his daughter to be the wife of King Solomon, who had succeeded his father, David, as ruler of the kingdom of Israel. At the same time, powerful priests of Amon in Thebes were in control of the south. With Egypt weakened, one group of foreigners after another—from Libya, Assyria and Persia—invaded the land.

Pharaohs of Dynasty 22, who had come from Libya, ruled from the city of Bubastis in the Delta. Bubastis was the center of worship of Bastet, the goddess of love and joy who took the form of a cat. This bronze cat, in a seated position, is dignified and graceful. She wears gold rings

Dynasty 26, about 665–525 B.C., British Museum

through her ears and nose and a fine necklace. A scarab is carved on her forehead.

Bastet was thought to accompany the boat of the sun god Ra through the regions of the night and to battle the serpent that was Ra's enemy. People wore charms in the form of cats to guard them against misfortune. Cats were kept in the temples, and when they died they were mummified and buried in cat cemeteries.

Ibises were also mummified and buried in cemeteries. This ibis, made of wood coated with gold, is hollow. It opens in back to hold the mummy of a dead bird.

Dynasty 30, about 380–340 B.C., The Brooklyn Museum, Charles Edwin Wilbour Fund

The long beak and talons are made of silver. It was believed that a long time ago there was no world. Then a heavenly bird, perhaps an ibis, laid an egg; out of it came Ra and the world began. The ibis was sacred to Thoth, god of wisdom. Thoth liked to take the form of an ibis so he could fly swiftly through the air with no one recognizing him. Killing an ibis was a crime punishable by death in Egypt.

The foreigners who invaded Egypt brought foreign ideas in dress, customs and art. But when the country became peaceful again, artists began to turn to the past for a pure Egyptian style. In the Late Period, sculptors carved figures in imitation of Old Kingdom statues. At left, a small figure of King Nectanebo II stands between the claws of the falcon god Horus, who is protecting him. The king is wearing the royal headcloth and the kilt of Old Kingdom Pharaohs. Horus wears the Double Crown, the headdress that stands for the unification of Egypt. It combines the tall crown of Upper Egypt with the flat crown of Lower Egypt.

Nectanebo II, who reigned during Dynasty 30, was the last Pharaoh of Egyptian blood to rule. During his reign the country was invaded by the Persians for the second time, then conquered by Alexander the Great of Macedonia. After Alexander's death, one of his generals became king of Egypt and was called Ptolemy I.

Thirteen rulers who followed him were also called Ptolemy.

Dynasty 30, The Metropolitan Museum of Art, Rogers Fund

The last of the Ptolemies to rule was a queen named Cleopatra VII. She was the daughter of Ptolemy XII and wife of Ptolemy XIII, who was also her brother. She ascended the throne at a time when the Romans, who were conquering most of the known world, were moving into Egypt. Cleopatra tried to win the Romans as allies and to keep Egypt independent. But the Roman army took over Egypt and made it a part of their empire.

The Ptolemies had adopted Egyptian religion and customs, as well as Egyptian styles of art. They built temples throughout the country in honor of Egyptian gods. The sunken relief at right, from the Temple of Hathor in Denderah in Upper Egypt, represents Cleopatra VII with her son, Caesarion. The queen is wearing the crown of the goddess Hathor.

Ptolemaic Period, about 330–30 B.C., photograph by John G. Ross

Egyptian art did not change very much in the course of the three thousand years that the Pharaohs reigned. Even after the Romans made Egypt a part of their empire, many of the old practices continued. Roman emperors represented themselves as Pharaohs and wrote their names in hieroglyphs. The Romans often combined Egyptian customs with their own ideas. They mummified their dead, and put flat wooden panels with realistic portraits over the faces of the deceased. This panel from the mummy of a young boy was painted with colors mixed with hot wax.

Islamic conquerors swept across North Africa, and the civilization of the ancient Egyptians was gradually forgotten. Then, about two hundred years ago, travelers began to discover the tombs, temples and towns of these people. The sand and dry air of the desert had preserved the mummies and the treasures that were buried with them. The ancient Egyptians wanted their lives to go on forever. Now, about five thousand years after the first Pharaoh, their images live on in their native land and in the museums of the world. It seems that their wish has come true.